W9-ACK-271

MAKING JEWELRY

By Dana Meachen Rau • Illustrated by Kathleen Petelinsek

CHERRY LAKE PUBLISHING • ANN ARBOR, MICHIGAN

CHERRY LAKE
Publishing

A NOTE TO ADULTS:
Please review the instructions for these craft projects before your children make them. Be sure to help them with any crafts you do not think they can safely conduct on their own.

A NOTE TO KIDS:
Be sure to ask an adult for help with these craft activities when you need it. Always put your safety first!

Published in the United States of America by Cherry Lake Publishing
Ann Arbor, Michigan
www.cherrylakepublishing.com

Content Adviser: Dr. Julia L. Hovanec, Professor of Art Education, Kutztown University, Kutztown, Pennsylvania

Photo Credits: Page 4, ©BestPhotoByMonikaGniot/Shutterstock, Inc.; page 6, ©Warren Price Photography/Shutterstock, Inc.; page 7, ©Jeremy Richards/Dreamstime.com; page 11, ©Julie Campbell/Dreamstime.com; pages 14, 20, 21, 22, 27, and 28, Dana Meachen Rau; page 32, Tania McNaboe

Library of Congress Cataloging-in-Publication Data
Rau, Dana Meachen, 1971–
    Making jewelry / by Dana Meachen Rau.
        pages cm — (How-to library. Crafts)
    Includes bibliographical references and index.
    ISBN 978-1-61080-475-2 (lib. bdg.) —
    ISBN 978-1-61080-562-9 (e-book) —
    ISBN 978-1-61080-649-7 (pbk.)
    1. Jewelry making—Juvenile literature. I. Title.
    TT212.R37 2012
    745.594'2--dc23   2012003186

Cherry Lake Publishing would like to acknowledge the work of The Partnership for 21st Century Skills. Please visit www.21stcenturyskills.org for more information.

Printed in the United States of America
Corporate Graphics Inc.
July 2012
CLFA11

TABLE OF CONTENTS

Art to Go!

Inspiration for art is everywhere.

Artists look for **inspiration** every day. They might look to sunsets, landscapes, or city skylines. They might look closely at the petals of a flower, the gears of a machine, or the shape of someone's nose. Such things inspire the artists to create art.

Some artists create art that hangs on a wall or sits on a table. Jewelry artists transform their ideas into something you can wear. Each piece of jewelry—whether it's a necklace, ring, or bracelet—is a creation that travels. It's art to go!

What inspires you? Perhaps you like observing nature or playing a sport. Maybe you have a favorite pet. Movies, music, and hobbies can be inspiring. Take your ideas and turn them into wearable art.

Keep a journal handy to capture all of your ideas.

IDEA JOURNAL
Artists often carry sketchbooks in their pockets or backpacks so they are ready to jot down ideas or make sketches. Try taking a small notebook with you on your travels. You might write or sketch an idea for a design that you can make into jewelry.

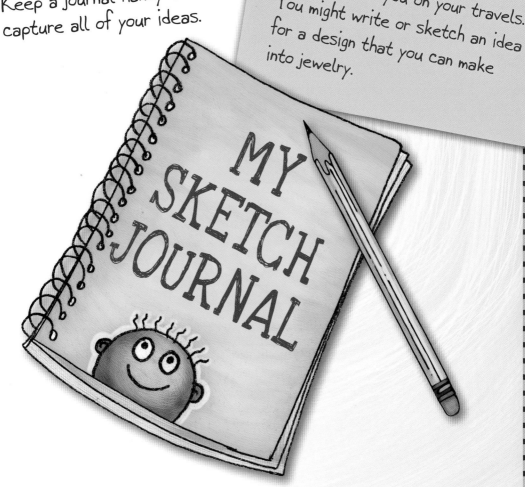

MY SKETCH JOURNAL

Decoration in History

Native Americans wore beaded decorations.

Throughout history, people have made things to help them survive. We made tools for cooking and hunting. We made shelters and clothing to keep warm. Besides the items we needed to live, we also created art to decorate our bodies and clothing.

Jewelry is an important part of **culture**. Long ago, artists transformed natural materials—such as wood, stone, and bone—into bracelets, necklaces, and other types of jewelry. Jewelry showed wealth, marked achievements, and played an important role in **rituals** and customs.

Ancient Egyptians, Greeks, Romans, Chinese, Africans, Native Americans, and many other cultures all made jewelry. Their traditions were handed down through many **generations**. Today, people still wear jewelry to decorate themselves just as they did thousands of years ago.

Bracelets, earrings, and other jewelry are important cultural traditions.

Basic Tools

So what can you use to make jewelry? Anything and everything! Jewelry combines many artistic **mediums**, such as metal, clay, paper, paint, and varnish. If you go into the jewelry section of a hobby store, you'll find many tools and supplies.

Metal

Artists use metal hardware such as pin backs, barrettes, earring hooks, and **clasps** to make their jewelry. These items might be made of steel or brass, or **plated** with gold or silver.

Beads

Hobby stores and bead shops sell beads made from metal, glass, plastic, clay, wood, and even paper. These beads come in many colors, sizes, and shapes.

Threads

Jewelry artists use different types of thread to string beads or weave designs. Thick threads called cords are made from leather, silk, or cotton. Other thread is clear or stretchy and made of plastic. Beading wire is made of metal.

Tools

You will need many tools and supplies for some of the projects in this book. Check out the materials list for each project before you get started. These are some general tools you will need:

- Tape measure and ruler—to measure your work
- Wire cutters and pliers—to cut and bend wire
- Tweezers—to help you pick up tiny beads
- Scissors—to cut cords

You may already have a lot of these supplies at home in a craft cabinet or a drawer. Your recycling bin may hold candy wrappers, plastic milk jugs, and old magazines that you can turn from trash into treasures. This is a great way to avoid wasting useful objects. All of the projects in this book reuse items that would have been thrown away.

OTHER MATERIALS

You don't have to stay in the jewelry aisle at a hobby store. You can also make jewelry from paper, wood, varnish, clay, and stickers. Visit a hardware store to find spray paint or duct tape. Fabric stores sell ribbon, feathers, and buttons.

Stringing Beads

There are three simple steps to making a project with beads.

Measuring Length

A tape measure is a **flexible** ruler. Use it to measure your wrist, ankle, or neck.

Designing the Pattern

A bead design tray can help you plan your pattern. You can buy one, but you could make your own. Here's how:

1. Fold a piece of 8 ½ x 11 inch (21.5 x 28 centimeter) card stock paper in half lengthwise.
2. About 1 inch from the center fold, fold the top flap of paper in the opposite direction.
3. About 1 inch from the center fold, fold the bottom flap of paper in the opposite direction, too.

You have created a V-shaped groove. This is where you can lay out your beads, switch them around, and experiment with your design. Keep a ruler handy. When you are happy with the final arrangement, measure the beads to make sure they match your needed measurement.

Stringing the Beads

Always cut your threads a couple of inches longer than your measurement. You'll need extra space on the ends to add a clasp or tie a knot. Place a piece of tape on one end of the string to keep your beads from falling off.

String the beads onto the other end one at a time from your tray. Often, you can just poke the thread through a bead's hole. But if the bead is small, you might need to use a long, thin beading needle.

Tie a knot or tape the end of your cord to keep the beads from falling off as you work.

Working with Wire

Wire comes in different **gauges**. The gauge is its thickness. Thinner wires have higher gauge numbers.

You'll need special tools to cut and shape wire. Always ask an adult to help you. Even if you are careful, wire can be sharp. You'll need a wire cutter that makes a completely flat, **flush** cut. You'll use round-nose pliers to make loops. Flat chain-nose pliers will allow you to hold and press loops closed.

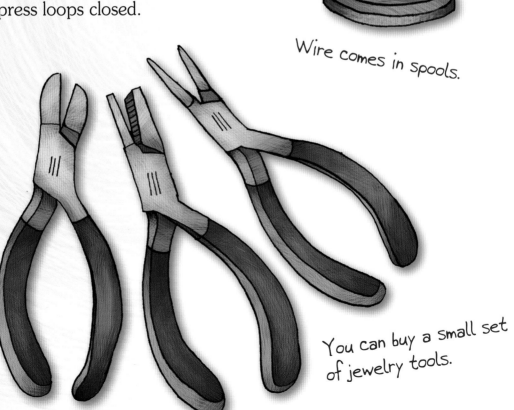

Wire comes in spools.

You can buy a small set of jewelry tools.

Here's how to make a loop with round-nose pliers:

1. Cut the tip of your wire with flush wire cutters.
2. Put the tip in the round-nose pliers and hold it in place. The tip should barely poke up on the top.
3. With your thumb, press and wrap the wire around the round tip of the pliers. You're wrapping the wire, not bending it with the pliers.
4. Readjust the pliers as you wrap the wire into a circle.

Always have an adult help you work with wire.

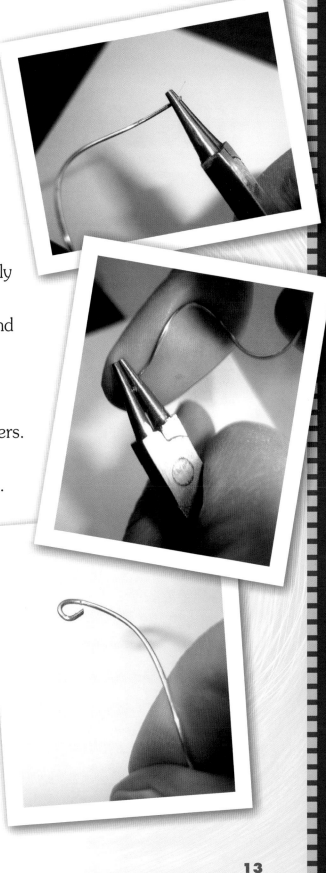

Nifty Knots

You can design your own interesting cords for a bracelet, anklet, or necklace. Here are some ways:

Basic Braid

1. Attach three cords of the same length together with an overhand knot. Clip the knot to the top of a sturdy book or clipboard.
2. Take the left-hand cord and place it over the cord in the middle.
3. Take the right-hand cord and place it over the new middle one.
4. Continue placing the cord from the left, then the right, over whichever cord is in the middle. Pull tightly as you braid. When you reach the end, secure the braid with another overhand knot.

Basic braid

Half Knot

1. You will need four cords. Two of them need to be three to four times longer than the other two. Attach all four together with an overhand knot. Arrange the two shorter cords in the center. The longer cords on the outsides will be the knotting cords.

2. Clip the knot to the top of the clipboard. Clip the two center cords to the bottom. The two knotting cords should move freely.

3. Remember these words, in order: over, over, under, through. Place the left cord over the center cords toward the right to create a loop on the left. Place the right cord over the left strand. Thread the right cord under the center cords and through the loop on the left side.

4. Pull the two knotting cord ends tightly to make a knot.

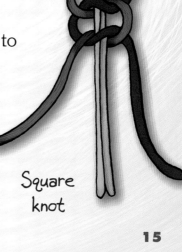

Half knot

Square Knot

1. Repeat steps 1 to 3 above to make a half knot.

2. To complete the square knot, remember this saying: under, under, over, through. Place the left cord under the center cords toward the right to create a loop on the left. Place the right cord under the left strand. Thread the right cord over the center cords and through the loop on the left side.

3. Pull the two knotting cord ends tightly to make a knot.

Square knot

FLAT AND SPIRAL
If you keep repeating the half knot, the cord will create a spiral stitch. If you complete the square knot, the cord will lie flat.

Decoupage

Decoupage (day-koo-PAHZH) is the art of cutting out images from paper and pasting them onto another surface, such as glass or wood. It is a great way to add images and color to a jewelry design.

Paper

Many hobby stores sell decorative papers. You may already have some interesting papers at home. Use leftover wrapping and tissue paper, images from magazines, or scraps of old maps. You could even use photos of your family and friends. You can cut out images with scissors or tear them out for a **jagged** edge.

Paste

You'll use varnish to paste your paper cutouts to a surface. Varnish is like glue. You first paste down the bottom side of your image. Then you brush over the image to seal it from the top. Water-based varnish is the easiest to clean up. It looks white when you brush it on, but it dries clear. You can find varnish at most craft stores.

Brush the varnish over the surface for a protective coating.

Here are the simple steps to decoupage:

1. Dip your paintbrush in the varnish.
2. Paint it onto your surface.
3. Place your paper flat onto the painted area.
4. Repaint over the top of the image.
5. If you want to, lay more papers on top, overlapping your first image.
6. Set your project aside to dry. Clean your brush with water.
7. Add more coats of varnish for a harder, more protective finish. For small projects, you may only need one or two coats.

Candy Wrapper Cuff Bracelet

Do you like to snack on sweet stuff? It's not healthy to bring a bag of candy with you everywhere you go. But it's fashionable to wear the wrapper!

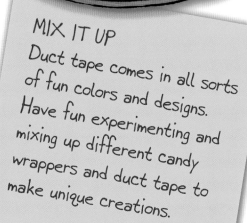

Materials

Scissors
Plastic milk jug
Duct tape (2 inches wide (5 cm))
Candy wrapper
Double-sided tape

MIX IT UP
Duct tape comes in all sorts of fun colors and designs. Have fun experimenting and mixing up different candy wrappers and duct tape to make unique creations.

Steps

1. Use scissors to cut a piece from a plastic milk jug about 1½ inches wide by 9 inches long (3.8 x 23 cm). Make sure your plastic strip is clean and dry.
2. Cut a piece of duct tape about 11 inches (28 cm) long and lay it flat on a table, sticky side up. Center the plastic strip on top. There should be about a quarter inch (0.6 cm) of tape showing on the top and bottom, and 1 inch (2.5 cm) on each side.

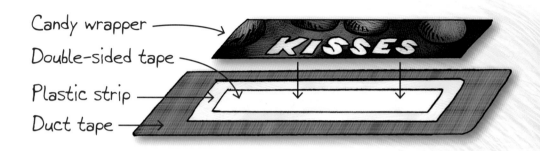

Candy wrapper

Double-sided tape

Plastic strip

Duct tape

3. Cut a strip out of a candy wrapper about 9 inches (23 cm) long and 1½ inches (3.8 cm) wide.

4. Place a piece of double-sided tape along the center of the plastic strip. Then lay the candy wrapper on top.

5. Fold up the duct tape along the bottom side and press to seal. Then fold and press the top strip of tape.

6. Fold over the duct tape on one end of the plastic strip. Repeat on the other end.

Fold over the top, bottom and both ends.

7. Bend the strip into a ring, wrapper side out, so the ends overlap about an inch (2.5 cm).

8. Cut a piece of duct tape about 3 inches (7.6 cm) long. Place it over the overlapped edges.

9. Fold over the duct tape on the top and bottom into the inside of your ring. Press it as flat as possible.

Secure the cuff with another piece of duct tape.

Party Pom-pom Ribbon Barrette

After your next birthday party, collect the ribbons from the presents. Use them to make another gift—a fun, festive barrette.

Use any colors of ribbon you wish.

Materials

Needle
Thread
About 5 yards (4.5 meters) of ¼-inch (0.6 cm) fabric ribbon
1 plain hair barrette
Scissors

Steps

1. Thread your needle with a piece of thread about 12 inches (30 cm) long. Knot the end.

Sew a running stitch along the whole piece of ribbon.

2. Cut a piece of ribbon 12 inches (30 cm) long.
3. Poke the needle up through one end of the ribbon and pull through. Then poke it down through the fabric and pull through again. This is called a running stitch. Continue sewing the running stitch up the whole length of the ribbon to the other end.

4. Pull on both ends of the thread so the ribbon zigzags and scrunches together.

5. Tie the two ends of the ribbon together tightly into a knot. Snip the ends of the thread. You have created a "bead" of ribbon.

6. Repeat steps 2 to 5 until you have made 15 ribbon beads.

7. Thread the needle with a piece of thread about 12 inches (30 cm) long. Instead of tying a knot at the end, secure it to one end of your barrette with a knot.

8. String three ribbon beads onto the thread.

9. Wrap the thread down through the top of the bar of the barrette and out the bottom. This will secure the beads onto the barrette.

10. String three more beads onto the thread. Again, wrap the thread around the bar of the barrette. Pull the thread tightly each time so that the beads are secure.

11. Continue until you run out of beads and reach the other end of the barrette. Secure the thread onto the barrette and tie a knot. Snip off the extra thread.

Swirly Spiral Earrings

Next time you use up all the paper in a spiral notebook, don't throw it away. Use the notebook's metal **coil** to make earrings!

Materials

Used spiral-bound notebook
Wire cutters
Round-nose pliers
2 wire ear hooks
Chain-nose pliers
Pencil
Ruler
About 24 plastic seed beads, any color

Instead of notebook wire, you can coil other craft wire to make these earrings, too.

Steps

1. Remove the spiral from the edge of the notebook.
2. Cut the spiral in half with the wire cutters. You should now have two pieces of wire, both with flush ends.
3. Create a loop at the end of one of the wire pieces. (*See pages 12–13 for steps.*) Thread this loop onto the loop of a wire ear hook.

Loop the coil onto the wire ear hooks.

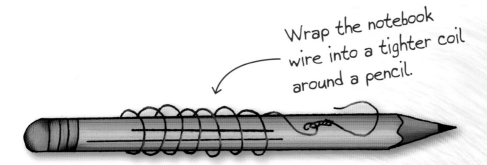

Wrap the notebook wire into a tighter coil around a pencil.

4. Tighten and close the wire loop with the chain-nose pliers so it won't slip off the ear hook.
5. Holding the ear hook in place at the top of a pencil, wrap the rest of the wire around and around the pencil. The wire is already coiled, but coiling it again will make a tighter spiral. Wrap until the coil measures 1½ inches (3.8 cm) long.
6. Thread 12 beads onto the wire.
7. With the round-nose pliers, make a loop at the bottom of the coil so the beads won't fall off. Tighten it with the chain-nose pliers.
8. Repeat steps 3 to 7 with the other piece of wire, to make a matching earring.

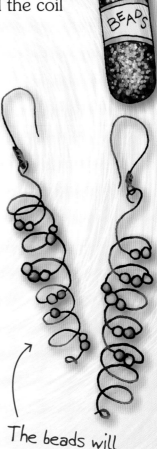

The beads will wind down the coil like a spiral slide.

EARRING RACERS!
The beads can move freely on the coils of your new earrings. For fun, move the beads to the top before putting the earrings on. See how long it takes them all to get to the bottom!

BEADS

23

Picture-Perfect Anklet

Flip through old magazines to find colorful photographs of flowers. Then turn them into a ring of blooms for your ankle. You can also cut out faces, letters to spell a word, or a mix of interesting colors or textures.

Materials

10 to 12 small square
   wooden beads
Permanent marker in the
   color of your choice
Scissors
Magazines
Paintbrush
Water-based varnish

Tape measure
10 to 12 round
   wooden beads
Elastic cord
Ruler
Tape

Steps

1. Color all six sides of the square wooden beads with the permanent marker. Set aside to fully dry.
2. Cut images from magazines into squares slightly smaller than the sides of your beads.

3. Dip your brush in the varnish and dab it onto the face of one of the beads.

4. Place a paper square onto the bead. Paint over the paper, flattening it as you brush on the varnish. Set the beads aside for about an hour to dry.

5. Measure your ankle with the tape measure.

6. Plan out your pattern on a bead tray. Alternate between the cube beads and the round ones. Check your pattern against your ankle measurement to make sure it is long enough.

7. Cut a length of elastic cord about 12 inches long. Place tape on one end to keep the beads from falling off.

8. String your beads onto the other end of the cord in the order you have laid them out on your tray.

9. Hold the two ends of cord together. Remove the tape and tie a square knot as close as you can to the two end beads.

10. Thread the remaining ends through a few of the beads on each side of the knot. Snip off the ends of extra thread.

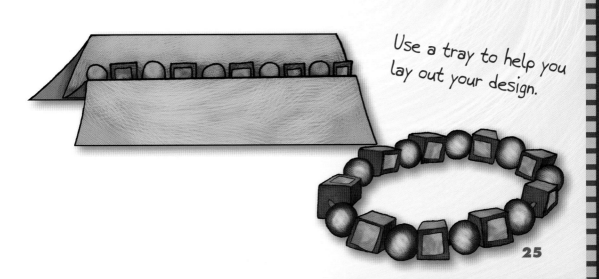

Use a tray to help you lay out your design.

Tied Together Forever Necklaces

Make necklaces for you and your best friend. Make them extra special by working on them together.

Materials

10 yards (9 m) of hemp cord
   in Color 1, and 10 yards
   (9 m) of hemp cord in
   Color 2 (enough to make
   2 necklaces)
Scissors

2 clips
Sturdy book or clipboard
2 metal washers
2 lobster clasps
Clear nail polish
Fine tip permanent marker

Steps

1. Take 5 yards (4.5 m) of Color 1 and 5 yards (4.5 m) of Color 2. Hold them together and fold them at 1 yard (0.9 m). Tie the folded cords in an overhand knot to make a small loop. The 1-yard (0.9 m) cords are the center cords. The other 4 yards (3.5 m) of cord are the knotting cords.

2. Clip the knot to the top of a clipboard or sturdy book. Clip the two center cords to the bottom.

3. Tie a half knot. (*See pages 14–15 for steps.*) Continue tying half knots until the piece measures 8 inches (20 cm) long. This is the midway point. As the piece spirals, you'll have to unclip and readjust it.

4. Place a washer on top of the center cords. Pull the cords up through the hole to make a loop.

5. Widen the loop. Thread the right knotting cord through the right side of the loop. Thread the left knotting cord through the left side of the loop.

6. As you tighten the loop, push the washer up to just below the last stitch.

Pull the center cords through the center of the washer, and thread the knotting cords into each side to hold the washer in place.

A lobster clasp holds your necklace together.

7. Tie a half knot at the base of the washer. Continue tying half knots for another 8 inches (20 cm).

8. Thread the two center cords into the hole on the lobster clasp. Push the clasp up to the base of the last stitch. Continue tying 3 more half knots to hold the clasp in place. Cut off the extra cords.

9. To help keep the knot from untying, coat the ends with some nail polish. Let the nail polish dry.

10. Repeat steps 1 to 9 to make a second necklace.

11. With the permanent marker, write "BEST" on the washer of one necklace and "FRIENDS" on the other.

12. Wear your necklace by attaching the clasp to the loop.

Share your creations with a friend.

BEST   FRIENDS

Endless Possibilities

Jewelry making is a craft with unlimited possibilities. There are many types of jewelry to make and a lot of materials to choose from. Mix that variety with your limitless imagination, and you can create beautiful art to wear.

So much of what people throw away isn't really trash. It can be reused to make wearable art. Look for materials you can use over again. Perhaps you can turn bottle caps into pins. Use old wooden game pieces as beads. Look for materials in nature, too. Collect shells to make a necklace or weave flower stems into a bracelet.

Work small, but think big. Your piece of jewelry doesn't just decorate you. It helps you express yourself and makes the world more beautiful, too!

Use your imagination and express yourself in a unique way.

Glossary

clasps (KLASPS) devices used to hold things together

coil (KOI-uhl) a spiral shape

culture (KUHL-chur) the art, traditions, and way of life of a group of people

flexible (FLEK-suh-buhl) able to bend

flush (FLUHSH) forming an even surface

gauges (GAY-jiz) thicknesses

generations (jen-uh-RAY-shuhnz) the people who live at a certain time

inspiration (in-spuh-RAY-shuhn) something that gives you a creative idea

jagged (JAG-id) rough

mediums (MEE-dee-uhmz) materials used to create art

plated (PLAY-tid) covered with a thin layer of a metal

rituals (RICH-oo-uhlz) special ceremonies

Tip

THREADING A NEEDLE
Sometimes it's hard to get the thread through the eye of a needle. Make sure you have good lighting. Trim the end of the thread so it is smooth. Poke it through the needle's eye. It may take a few tries.

Pull the thread through and join the threaded end with the other end. Tie the two ends together in an overhand knot. The thread will be doubled as you sew, making it stronger. It will also keep the needle from unthreading while you work.

For More Information

Books

Di Salle, Rachel, and Ellen Warwick. *Junk Drawer Jewelry*. Toronto: Kids Can Press, 2006.

Kenney, Karen Latchana. *Super Simple Jewelry*. Edina, MN: Abdo Publishing Company, 2010.

Newcomb, Rain. *The Girls' World Book of Jewelry*. New York: Lark Books, 2004.

Packham, Jo. *Artful Jewelry*. San Francisco: Chronicle Books, 2009.

Scheunemann, Pam. *Cool Beaded Jewelry*. Edina, MN: Abdo Publishing Company, 2005.

Web Sites

American Museum of Natural History: Totems to Turquoise

www.amnh.org/exhibitions/totems

Check out some Native American jewelry to get ideas for your own projects.

Disney Family Fun: All Jewelry

http://familyfun.go.com/crafts/crafts-by-type/jewelry-accessories/ jewelry-crafts

Follow along with these projects to create even more jewelry.

National Gallery of Art: The Art Zone

www.nga.gov/kids/zone/zone.htm

Look at different kinds of art to get inspiration for your projects.

Index

About the Author

Dana Meachen Rau is the author of more than 300 books for children on many topics, including science, history, cooking, and crafts. She creates, experiments, researches, and writes from her home office in Burlington, Connecticut.